LISTEN TO WH...
LEADERS HAV...
DIRTY WORDS!

"Do you have an hour to change your life? That is all it takes to read Randy Lennon's thought-provoking book, The Dirty Words. Simply changing the words you use can powerfully change the direction of your life! Just like a small metal coupling, not much larger than a person's hand, can alter the course of a large train to a destination a thousand miles away in the matter of a day, so can a reader of this book alter their course by shifting small words. They can help you reach the destinations you want to go far from where you are. Who "can't" afford an hour for that?"

- Adrian Bohach
CEO of Enterprise4Good

"The Dirty Words is absolutely wonderful. I can easily see it becoming a welcome reference piece for people in their quest to become better people (a thankfully growing community)! I found it truly enthralling from beginning to end. Smart, funny, endearing. The format, the pace, the tone, and the lack of fluff all combine to make it a very attractive overall presentation. The matter-of-fact approach to persuasion is a very cunning method and I love it. It gets right to the point and is indisputable."

- Matthew Jensen
Founder & CEO of Maxogram Media Inc.

"Randy Lennon helps us explore the simple powerful truths about the impact of our words. There are not enough books on this subject, and it would be wonderful if this book were part of a curriculum which was taught in schools, to teachers, to children and to parents alike. Once we know better, it becomes easier to make a positive impact with word choices. Leaders in all fields of business, politics and social movements are also taking notice as it is becoming increasingly important to choose your words wisely. You will enjoy a gamut of surprises as you read and realize that there is so much more to consider on the subject of word choice and psychology."

- Valerie Maltese
Loveographer (Co-writer of personal love stories.) Certified Life Cycle Celebrant, ACTRA Performer, TESOL certified, Minister with CIMM

"I was going to let Randy know that I probably can't read his book right now because I don't have time. But that I would, at the very least, try. I was going to wish him well and hope the venture far exceeds his expectations. Then I decided, I love Randy, he has been there for me - so I will take the time to read The Dirty Words. Because I can and not because I should. I quit 'shoulding' on myself years ago. I am glad that I can and I will because The Dirty Words is a compelling reminder that, in a 140-character world where communication by text seems to trump all, words matter more now than ever!

The Dirty Words is a textbook for the 140-character universe. I would make it mandatory reading for anyone who ever intends to hit send again."
- Ritch Winter
NHL Hockey Agent and founder of the Business of Hockey Institute

"I have known Randy Lennon for many years and worked with him on many projects! The Dirty Words is a Randy I didn't know!

I find this to be a very interesting read reflecting Randy's years of practical experience dealing with real people. It is both very thoughtful and thought provoking. It is inspirational, insightful, helpful, very useful, educational, valuable and discussable. It is also very topical in these very interesting, different and challenging times."
- John P.C. Elson,
P.ENG, former Chairman of Athabasca University

"I would like to recommend Randy Lennon's The Dirty Words to a wide audience for its fundamental wisdom from thought leaders going back centuries. Randy draws from life to anchor his positions in reality and to inspire with integrity. I can picture the conversations that this will stimulate at the family tables. Thank you, Randy!"
- Lauren Nickel
ICD.D, Board Director and Advisor to several companies.

"Reading Ready Lennon's book, The Dirty Words, will save you 10 years of personal development training. (And thousands of dollars). His style is fun and upbeat to read and carries a powerful message. Simply exchange the 7 "dirty words" (disempowering words) for words that bring truth and impact. I happened to read 'The Dirty Words' when I was feeling in a depressive down cycle that I was having difficulty shaking. I decided to apply the program and was surprised how quickly my mood changed and my positive energy returned.

It's simply the fastest easy-to-apply, change-your-life- for-the-better manual out there."

- Kirei Yasunori
Owner, Evolved Health

"Language is important, it carries weight and can have a major influence, on ourselves and on others.

Randy Lennon's book is full of great examples of how the words we choose can and often do impact our attitudes, the feelings we create and what is possible. Speaking with intention, clarity and control is within all of us. Randy's book is entertaining, thought provoking and memorable. He provides every one of his readers with powerful reasons to eliminate the 'dirty words' from our vocabulary and replace them with words that serve us and others well."

- Noelle Leemburg
Founder bSavvy, Inc and Co-Founder of
The Resilient Mind

"Randy Lennon's book hits upon a striking way to examine one's life and word choices to make an immediate impact on yourself and your interactions with friends, associates, lovers, spouses and family. The book is a quick read that is filled with important points to improve your communication skills and happiness as you navigate through this complicated thing we call life."

- Gary Sommers – Entrepreneur, Husband and Father

THE DIRTY WORDS

Change Your Language, Change Your Life

The Official Companion Book to
The Questions Experience

By Randy Lennon

THEQUESTIONSEXPERIENCE.COM

Published by
Hyperspace Internet Technologies, Inc. Publishing Division
1308 Stockton Hill Road, Suite A177
Kingman, AZ 86401
hyperspaceit.com

The Dirty Words:
Change Your Language, Change Your Life
Copyright © 2020 by Randy Lennon
Cover design by Hyperspace Internet Technologies, Inc.

All rights reserved. No part of this book may be used or reproduced in any manner whatsoever without written permission except in the case of brief quotations embodied in critical articles and reviews.
For information please address Randy Lennon.
randy@randylennonmedia.com

Library of Congress Control Number: 2020911798
ISBN (e-book): 978-0-578-71888-0
ISBN (paperback): 978-0-578-71889-7

This book is dedicated to Dee, Dave,
Mike and Chris with all my love.

"Words have a magical power. They can either bring the greatest happiness or the deepest despair."
- Sigmund Freud

"Throughout human history, our greatest leaders and thinkers have used the power of words to transform our emotions, to enlist us in their causes, and to shape the course of destiny. Words can not only create emotions, they create actions. And from our actions flow the results of our lives."
- Tony Robbins

"If we understood the power of our thoughts, we would guard them more closely. If we understood the awesome power of our words, we would prefer silence to almost anything negative. In our thoughts and words, we create our own weaknesses and our own strengths. Our limitations and joys begin in our hearts. We can always replace negative with positive."
- Betty Eadie

"Be sure to taste your words before you spit them out."
– Anonymous

FOREWORD

Randy Lennon brings insight and awareness to the reader in this easy-to-read and entertaining book, "The Dirty Words". In a world where you can turn on the television or peruse social media at will, it is often too easy to be a voyeur of negativity, savour others' misfortune or gloss over some of the truly wonderful events that are happening around the world.

As a graduate of the "School of Hard Knocks," Randy has chosen to pass on some of his experience and wisdom in a way that is easy to understand and identify with. We all use the Dirty Words in everyday life as reasons NOT to see and do the positive in life — "I would do this BUT".

By simply drawing these words and statements to the attention of the reader Randy has given you the tools to change your life and go from dwelling on the negative to extolling the virtue of every situation. Well done Randy!

Dr. Lyle Oberg
Medical Doctor, Business Leader, Board Director of several companies, and Innovator, Former Minister of Finance, Minister of Learning, Minister of Infrastructure and Transportation, and Minister of Social Services of The Province of Alberta, Canada

INTRODUCTION

Apparently, most readers don't bother with the introduction so let me start off by saying, "thank you for being here." It's actually very humbling to contemplate someone, you in this case, taking your valuable time to read this book. Being my first published book, it's even more especially an honour and a delight to invite you into my world.

The Dirty Words concept grew out of a desire to get workshop registrants prepared to write down their answers to "The Questions." And what are The Questions, you ask? Good question, as they say! They are eight amazing Questions that were divinely given to me one afternoon in the late 90's as I prepared a "questionnaire" to include in a package to be sent to participants in an experiential workshop that I was planning to facilitate. The idea was for me to get a sense of what these workshop attendees wanted to get out of their experience. Where were they at in their life, in their spiritual journey? I felt strongly that if I could get them to answer a few key questions that I would have a better understanding of how to guide them through and get the most value out of the weekend workshop.

When I called each of the participants in advance and we discussed their answers to the eight questions, the power of The Questions themselves was suddenly revealed. With each person and each question, I found

The Dirty Words

myself challenging them on their answers, probing further and asking them more questions. It suddenly became a phenomenal opportunity for growth and deep reflection as The Questions seemed to guide us down a path of new awakenings and breakthroughs. The tears flowed, answers were re-considered, evaluated, re-crafted and often times completely changed from relatively lame answers to totally empowering answers. Working with these amazing eight Questions was suddenly and obviously not only a delight, but a calling.

The weekend workshop never took place. Instead, I started thinking about how powerful writing down answers to deep, direct, and compelling Questions can be and how the words we choose are so critical to the reality we create for ourselves. The Dirty Words developed into a very fun and impactful first part of what eventually became The Questions Experience workshop. And as amazing as the awakenings and breakthroughs were for the hundreds of people who either attended the workshop or received one-on-one coaching around their answers to The Questions, years later people continued to reach out to me about the lasting impact that The Dirty Words portion of the workshop had on them. Being aware of these insidious yet widely prevalent words in our common language and how disempowering and even damaging they can be, has been a lasting gift for many people. So, around the Christmas holidays in 2017, I decided to write this book.

My intention with this book, as with the Dirty Words portion of The Questions Experience workshop, is to have some fun and laughter while exploring an important

Introduction

subject that can be deeply impactful, and even change your life. Yes, being more aware of the vital importance of the words you choose (and the fact that you are indeed "at choice" in every word you say) and their potentially enormous impact on everyone around you, is an eye opener to say the least for most people in Dirty Word workshops. Beginning to understand how pervasive "sloppy language" is in our society and what a devastating impact it has on others is vital. What's really stunning is to begin to understand what a destructive impact our own words can have on ourselves!

I invite you to really dig into this short book. It's a "light read" and yet there is a lot here to really let sink in.

Thank you for your commitment to being a better person that has prompted you to open this book.

Randy Lennon
July 2020

CONTENTS

FOREWORD xiii

INTRODUCTION xv

Chapter 1 When Did You Learn to Swear? 1

Chapter 2 The Power of the Spoken Word 7

Chapter 3 A Culture of Victimhood 13

Chapter 4 The "Get To" Housekeeper 19

Chapter 5 "SHOULDing" All Over Yourself 29

Chapter 6 I Love You BUT 33

Chapter 7 I'll TRY to Be There 37

Chapter 8 I CAN'T 41

Chapter 9 I HOPE It Works Out for You 45

Chapter 11 I WISH I Could Help 49

Chapter 12 Speaking with Intention and Clarity 51

Chapter 13 Programming the Subconscious Mind 55

Chapter 14 A Real-Life Superhero 59

EPILOGUE 67

ACKNOWLEDGMENTS 69

ABOUT THE AUTHOR 71

CHAPTER 1

WHEN DID YOU LEARN TO SWEAR?

How old were you when you learned to swear? At age 61 I'm not sure of the answer for myself and I distinctly remember the answer for my son, Mike. He was 3 years old.

It was the Christmas season, and I was back in my hometown of Edmonton, Alberta in Canada to spend time with my Mom, Dad, siblings, their families, and some extended family visiting from out of town. I was pretty excited to invite everyone for an afternoon get together at the beautiful Westin Hotel where I had managed to score the "Royal Suite" (apparently at some point along the way none other than the Queen of England had stayed in this room).

At the time, I was living one of my many dreams by producing and co-hosting a comedy sports talk radio show on a popular AM radio station in Vancouver, BC. I had managed to barter some advertising time on the show in exchange for a few nights in this expansive hotel suite (which I'm pretty certain would have been vacant over the holidays at the asking price of $2,000 per night) and was pretty excited to host a family pre-Christmas event.

The Dirty Words

Everyone was there, all dressed up for Christmas. All the Lennon's, my wife Dee's mom and sister, and some extended family from out of town. Including kids, there were probably 25 or 30 people. We were all enjoying light conversation, festive finger food, and spirits. A lovely family event.

All of a sudden, out of the "blue" (and no pun intended here) little 3-year-old Michael Lennon blurted out in a rather loud voice a single syllable word that starts with "f," ends with "k" and is a common colloquialism for "fornication." As the room quieted and everyone looked over, he seemed to relish in the attention and said it again….. and again, and again.

Somewhat horrified, my wife looked at me and I looked at her. I believe we had the same simultaneous thought along the lines of, "I can't believe he picked that up from you!"

Most interesting to me was that little Mike was barely talking at all yet, and certainly very quiet and reserved. So, this particular outburst of profanity was a complete surprise, and not a particularly pleasant one.

What are you supposed to do as a parent in such a scenario? I'm not sure there is a correct answer to that question. I hadn't read any parenting books at that time and although my wife certainly had studied parenting since she was a teenager, I don't believe any brilliant responses popped into either of our heads. There were a few muffled, restrained chuckles. We both smiled uncomfortably to our family members as if to silently say, "oh my goodness, we're not sure where that came from and kids are cute at times aren't they?" ….. or something along those lines.

When did you first learn to swear? Whether on the playground, learning from an older sibling, or being born that way, (as was obviously the case with our little Mike … ha ha) the energy of those special, forbidden, dirty words became clear for all of us at some point along the way. We learned those words, sometimes what they actually meant, and we particularly learned where and when their use was acceptable and completely unacceptable.

Regardless of our upbringing, our social class, our religion or lack thereof, swear words were a part of all our lives. We may have had longer or shorter lists of dirty words, and one could debate what words were included.

I distinctly remember what at the time seemed like a very exciting debate with my Aunt Shirley on the farm in Sandy Lake, Manitoba where I spent many summers as a kid, about whether or not "shit" should be on the forbidden dirty words list.

Her position was that there really was no other proper descriptive and definitive word for …. well, you know … shit. Cow pie didn't cut it for her. Poop seemed somehow childish and dung didn't work for her either. The word feces I certainly wasn't aware of at the time and Aunt Shirley may not have been either so that was not discussed. So, at age 9, I and my aunt came to the understanding that shit was ok. She was also fine with crap, both of which were off the table, so to speak, back in perhaps the more conservative Lennon household in Edmonton. We didn't discuss the f word.

Nonetheless, I didn't test out using the word shit when I got back home. We weren't allowed to swear at our house, and I never, ever heard my parents swear. It wasn't a particularly religious home, and in retrospect I think my parents in the 60's and early 70's were rather progressive in their thinking. Notwithstanding, swearing was a definite no no.

At school, well that was a different story. By the time I got to junior high I became well aware of the majority of *The Seven Words You Can't Say On Television,* according to comedian George Carlin. It was a classic and very funny monologue that may seem silly today as at least 6 of the 7 are now commonly used on TV, at least networks like HBO. Even on the main network late night talk shows swearing is now common, although the actual sounds are "bleeped" out, and of course remain clear to the audience.

So, to quote another even more famous comedian than George Carlin, Jerry Seinfeld: "What is the deal with swearing?"

Our society has developed over time a relatively short list of dirty words. Words that often have multiple meanings and are clearly not appropriate in most settings. They are at their core disrespectful, irreverent, rude and fundamentally vulgar. Carlin's seven words (shit, piss, fuck, cunt, cocksucker, motherfucker, and tits) reference sex acts, body parts and bodily functions. And then there are the religious based dirty words that take the Lord's name in vain.

Yes, we all learned these words. And we also learned where and where not to use them. Some of us may have decided never to use any of these words. Some use them virtually all the time. I've been on construction sites and in locker rooms where certain of these words seemed to be used in every sentence of conversation, sometimes more than once per sentence.

For most people, the dirty words are saved for certain situations where we really want to make an impact. Most of us, when we get really, really angry or upset, will resort to foul language to express our frustration, distress, distain, and even hatred. There's no doubt these words can be used like weapons and can provoke dangerous, sometimes disastrous responses and reactions. Fights have broken out, guns have been drawn, and yes people have died as a direct result of indiscriminate use of dirty words.

"Them's fightin' words," is one quote from many an old-time western movie.

And then there are very strategically used dirty words in otherwise sophisticated settings. The carefully, and calmly dropped f-bomb in a Fortune 500 boardroom as part of negotiation or positioning strategy; the c-word shockingly uttered on girls' night out among upwardly mobile moms after a few too many glasses of wine; the soft-spoken point of emphasis spoken by the judge after prosecutor and defense counsel have approached the bench.

Yes, dirty words make for a fascinating exploration of the human condition.

One thing is certain, we all learn where and when to use the dirty words, sometimes the hard way. We are aware of them, are offended or even appalled by their use in certain situations and find them perfectly acceptable or even comical in other situations.

The dirty words have their place.

And this book is not about those dirty words. This book is about a whole other set of dirty words that we don't think of as dirty at all. They are all over our everyday language. It's fair to say they are rampant in our conversations, our books, television, radio, social media, and of course, all over the Internet. These dirty words permeate all aspects of our communication and are a general menace to effective communication, relationship building, and virtually all aspects of building functional communities and societies on the planet.

These new dirty words really have no place in our language. And it's time to eliminate them from our vocabularies.

CHAPTER 2

THE POWER OF THE SPOKEN WORD

Human history is full of proclamations.

"We will send a man to the surface of the moon and bring him back safely to earth before this decade is out." Those were the words of President John F. Kennedy in a famous speech in 1961. Now, admittedly he was the President of the United States, arguably the most powerful nation on the earth and perhaps the man on the planet with the most resources at his disposal. Still, it was a pretty bold proclamation.

Especially when you consider that at the time he made that statement, no one had any real idea how to do it, how much it could cost, where the money would come from, and whether it was even possible. It's safe to say that the technology simply did not exist at that time to achieve what he was saying was going to happen.

And it's also safe to say that it would not have happened had he not said it.

I'll never forget that day in July of 1969. My beloved Uncle Ned was part of a Barbershop Singing Group in Edmonton and they were putting on a big show at the Jubilee Auditorium, a soft seater venue of 3,000 seats built to celebrate the 50th jubilee anniversary of the Province of Alberta. The identical building was constructed in Calgary as well and they're both still in use well past the Province's centennial celebrations in 2005. It was pretty exciting to be behind the scenes helping with the show as a 12-year-old boy who was destined to be an impresario.

Yet, the big show at the Jubilee Auditorium took a back seat to a live television show that everyone rushed home to gather around the TV to see. Uncle Ned was one of the few I knew who had a colour TV at the time, yet this event was being broadcast in black and white. There we were, eyes glued to the tube as we watched NASA Astronaut Neil Armstrong descend from the Apollo 11 lunar landing vehicle to broadcast his famous words, "That's one small step for man (he meant to say "a man") and one giant leap for mankind."

President Kennedy's bold, perhaps even audacious proclamation had come to fruition. And so it can be said for every major breakthrough achievement in human history. Every invention, innovation, technological advancement, and progression of any kind is always, without exception, the result of someone having a vision and at some point, in some way, voicing that vision.

The power of the spoken word.

All great leaders in human history have made proclamations. They imagine what can be, and then speak their vision.

What proclamations have you made in your life?

"I'm going to marry her."

"I'm going to get that job."

"I'm going to make the team."

"I'm going to get my degree."

"I'm going to be an actor."

"I'm going to be a doctor."

"I'm going to make it happen."

"I'm going to run a marathon."

"I'm in charge here."

It's certainly safe to say that not all proclamations come to fruition. And it's also safe to say that nothing happens or is created until someone speaks.

What building was ever built without someone saying, "I think we will build on that site"?

What politician ever won an election without first proclaiming, "I am running for office"?

What charitable organization was ever built without someone taking a stand and saying, "It's time to step up and do something about this situation"?

And then there are the commands, demands, and simple instructions that allow civilization to function and literally build our world. Of course, these are usually put in the form of the written word as well AND again, nothing happens without someone speaking.

Think about all of the words you say in a day. How often are you making proclamations? And how many of those proclamations do you even realize are proclamations, literally shaping your world? Those proclamations are having a huge impact on not only all of the people in your life, those proclamations are having a huge impact on you!

What impact does the spoken word have? I can make a case that nothing that exists in the material world has more impact that the spoken word. And when we look at the spiritual world, what is the basis of all Christian teachings? The answer is, "The Word." The word of God… as spoken by Jesus Christ, his apostles, and then all the pastors and preachers since Christ was born.

In all religions faith in a higher power is expressed many ways, and none more powerful than through the spoken word.

The Power of the Spoken Word

The great orators have always been able to unite the people of this world both for good and evil. There is no doubt Adolf Hitler chose his words very carefully, as did Martin Luther King. Ghandi defeated arguably the world's strongest army armed only with his words.

I challenge you to look around you and listen. Become aware of the power of the spoken word in your life. What do you choose to listen to and who do you listen to? And how do those words affect you, your loved ones, and the world around you?

Powerful, yes. And no words have more power and impact on your life and the lives of your loved ones than your own words. Are you choosing them carefully and do you really understand the impact these words can and do have? Most of us are guilty of being dangerously careless with our words. And not just in the ways that come to mind.

CHAPTER 3

A CULTURE OF VICTIMHOOD

Do you realize that you are always "at choice?" Most of us do not fully understand and appreciate what it means to be *at choice*.

Henry David Thoreau wrote, "The mass of men lead lives of quiet desperation." It's certainly a sad and even hopeless view of life. Yet it resonates for all of us at some point along our way. Depression, fear and anxiety are rampant in our ever more complex world. As society evolves and technology continues to have an exponentially greater impact on our day to day lives, it's not surprising that we can lose connection with our true selves and feel, simply, out of control.

Have you ever felt buffeted through life? Are you bounced around like a lottery ball or a bumper car or a pin ball? As children we are completely at the mercy of our parents or whomever looks after us. As we grow into adulthood, we make a gradual transition to taking over control of our own lives. For many, it's not so gradual and can be the source of trauma that haunts us throughout our lives.

Some never fully transition into adulthood and never come to a true understanding that we are all, always at choice. We believe someone else is always in control. Not only do we deny that we are always "at choice", we feel we have no choice at all.

We are victims.

We are victims of circumstance. We are victims of poverty. We are victims of discrimination. We are victims of bullies. We are victims of crime. We are victims of abuse. We are victims of government. We are victims of success. We are victims of prejudice. We are victims of religion. We are victims of inequality. We are victims of husbands. We are victims of wives. We are victims of addiction. We are victims of tyrants. We are victims of climate change. We are victims of disease. And of course, we are victims of our parents… and so on.

We are living increasingly in a culture of victimhood. The USA, already the most litigious culture on the planet, becomes even more litigious as we self-righteously scramble to right every wrong and compensate every victim.

We go to great lengths to protect ourselves and our children from feeling bad and in doing so, make that transition to adulthood, control, discipline and responsibility even more of a challenge.

We are addicted to rights without the balance of responsibility.

A Culture of Victimhood

Our words feed into this cultural malaise. And we are for the most part, unaware of how certain words that are common, even pervasive in our language, are not only not serving us, these words are damaging us and those around us who are listening. Most of all, these words harm us. They disempower us. We allow them to inflict the most damage on ourselves.

We do not realize that we are always at choice.

"Everything happens for a reason and it serves me."

"It does not matter what happens."

Do these two statements jar you? Or do you think you believe them?

I'll take it a step further:

"It NEVER matters what happens."

Now I've got your attention. "Of course," you say, "it matters what happens! It matters to me when things go wrong. It matters when I face challenges. It matters when someone I love gets cancer. It matters when someone dies. OF COURSE IT MATTERS WHAT HAPPENS!"

Your statements are true and all part of our victim culture, IF that's what you choose to believe. And, you are always at choice.

What if I add these words to complete the philosophy?

"It NEVER matters what happens. It ONLY matters what you make it mean and how you choose to respond."

This may seem like a radical view of life. The fact is – it is the only sane way to look at life. Any other way is a form of insanity.

We must come to the realization that our life is lived in the present moment and we can have absolutely no impact, whatsoever, in any way, shape or form on what has already occurred. The past is history, the future is a mystery, right now is a gift... that's why we call it "the present."

What happens is not the basis on which to live our lives. If we are going to allow our life to be run by what happens, we are completely giving up our responsibility to be happy, to live gracefully, peacefully and with love in our hearts.

To do anything but fully accept what has happened is a form of insanity.

It is up to us to accept what has happened, in every single moment. It is up to us to decide what we are going to make it mean, and then decide how we are going to respond.

That is a recipe for sanity and living an empowered life. It's the opposite of being a victim.

So, let's take a closer look. Bad things do happen. We live in a world of good AND evil. Mother Nature provides an absolutely beautiful and truly awesome environment for us to live. And she can also kill us.

I am not suggesting that bad things aren't going to happen. The question is: "Are bad things happening TO us, or are they just happening?"

When we live by the philosophy that everything happens for a reason and it serves me, we are not only living in faith, we are living a life of truly being at choice. Christians believe that God granted us free will, yet at the same time we are all part of a greater plan. The simple answer when we face adversity or bad things are happening is to "Turn it over to God."

That's a great answer. And after turning it over to God, what do we do? The answer is to make a decision about our interpretation of events. We get to determine the meaning to us of what has happened. How are we going to interpret what has happened, or even is happening? Are we going to depend on our belief that everything happens for a reason and it serves me? If so, we will seek an interpretation that serves us and respond appropriately.

When it's REALLY bad, it can be very difficult and sometimes seemingly impossible to find the positive interpretation. How can losing a child, for example, possibly be for a reason and how can it possibly serve us? God help me, I have not faced that circumstance. Many have never fully recovered. Their grief never truly subsides.

The Dirty Words

One of the ways a parent deals with losing a child is through acceptance. As with every bad thing that happens, from a minor annoyance to a horrible tragedy, the undeniable fact is that it has already happened. It is in the past and cannot be changed. And we truly DO get to choose what to make it mean. And how we are going to respond.

Many of us have had the experience of realizing, later down the road, how something that seemed to be the worst thing that could happen at the time actually turned out to be a good thing. Sometimes the worst disaster turns out to be the best thing that ever happened. As difficult as it may be, it is always best to look for what may be the good that can come out of a bad scenario.

Many of us, in our victim culture, turn even minor annoyances into tragedies. By believing we are out of control, our lives are unmanageable, and that bad stuff is always happening "to" us, and we are unable to cope. We have no idea that we can change what we make things mean. We have no idea that we can decide how to respond, not just react.

We don't know we are at choice. And then the "dirty words" spew out of our cake holes.

CHAPTER 4

THE "GET TO" HOUSEKEEPER

Now we begin our journey of identifying, exploring their damaging nature, and eliminating the "Dirty Words" from our vocabulary. In doing so, we will make simple, yet profound changes in our language that can literally change everything.

A construction laborer who decides to go back to school gets re-trained in a new profession and must adapt to a boardroom from a construction site environment. She gets to ditch her foul language, which was perfectly acceptable with her construction peers. Those seven words you can't say on TV no longer serve her in her new role as a Manager of Human Resources. Or, the criminal turned pastor gets to change up the vocabulary in making a successful transition from prison to Church. And you get to simply stop using every day, simple words that disempower you. Words that unknowingly position you as a victim. Words that are counterproductive and actually cause people to resent you. Words that fuel an epidemic of miscommunication and misunderstanding. Words that are the enemy of clarity.

These are the new "Dirty Words".

The Dirty Words

Dirty Word #1 –
Have to

Substitute Words –
Going to
Will do

BEST SUBSTITUTE –
Get to

There are two kinds of housekeepers at hotels around the world. There is the "have to" housekeeper and the "get to" housekeeper.

One is grouchy, hates her life, misses work a lot because she gets sick frequently. She struggles to make ends meet. She is in and out of bad relationships. She battles with anxiety and depression and she drinks too much.

The other is an absolute delight to be around. She literally lights up the hotel room when she walks in. She is happily married to a wonderful man, is very proud of her three adult children and loves when her two grandchildren come to visit.

Both of these women clean toilets for a living. The first is a "have to" person and the second is a "get to" person.

Everyone uses the toilet. Every toilet gets dirty and requires cleaning. All of us either clean our toilets or we make arrangements for someone else to do it for us. It's

The "Get To" Housekeeper

that simple. As regards toilet cleaning, we are always at choice.

The first housekeeper does not realize that she is at choice. She is buffeted around by life. She feels her life is out of control. And, it IS out of control because she is making a choice to be a victim. She has a very "foul" mouth and can be heard "swearing" often:

"I have to go to work."

"I have to get up early."

"I have to be on time."

"I have to deal with my crappy boyfriend."

"I have to call my mother."

"I have to take the bus to work."

"I have to figure out how to live on minimum wage."

"I have to put on this ugly uniform."

"I have to clean toilets all day."

The second housekeeper has made one simple change in her language. She has eliminated one dirty word (phrase actually) and replaced it with a substitute word (phrase). Here's how she talks:

"I get to go to work."

"I get to get up early."

"I get to be on time."

"I get to deal with my grumpy husband." (chuckle to herself)

"I get to call my mother."

"I get to take the bus to work."

"I get to figure out how to live on minimum wage."

"I get to put on this ugly uniform." (chuckle to herself)

"I get to clean toilets all day." (chuckle to herself)

I am married to a woman who absolutely loves cleaning. I'm pretty sure even she does not really like to clean the toilets. And most of us, at one time or another, found ourselves in the situation where we made a decision to clean the toilet. Let's be clear, there is always a choice. If you are not able to convince, coerce, or hire someone else to do it, you can also choose to just let the toilet be dirty.

So, for whatever reason, we decide to clean the toilet. Guess what? At that point, why on earth would we say to anyone, especially to ourselves, that we "have to" clean the toilet?

The "Get To" Housekeeper

For one thing, we would be lying, because we don't have to. For another, we would be acting as if someone else is running our life. Some other person, or greater force, or higher power is inflicting his, her, or its will on us and FORCING us to do this awful, and smelly task. We would be surrendering to victimhood. "Oh, poor me, I HAVE TO clean the toilet!"

We can certainly be more honest and simply say, "I'm going to clean the toilet," or, "I'm choosing to clean the toilet." The perfect replacement phrase is actually "I get to clean the toilet." That will bring a smile to your face and even a chuckle to yourself because of the ironic nature of the statement.

And, it works! It's amazing actually.

Tony Robbins taught me in 1990 the power of "changing your state." He suggested that we all have many, many opportunities each day to completely change our state from being frustrated, grumpy, depressed, even angry, by simply changing the answer to a question we get asked all day long: "How are you?" We have a choice at that moment to choose our words carefully.

Now, let's be clear. This doesn't have to be about an honest answer because 9 times out of 10 the person asking doesn't really want to know how you actually are. It's just a normal form of greeting. And they especially don't want to know how you are if it's not good. No, this is simply a social custom that provides a fantastic opportunity for you to get into a habit of being and feeling great every time you get asked that question.

Most of us have a standard answer.

"I'm ok."

"I'm good." (which is actually poor grammar)

"Not bad."

"Not too bad." (which actually means bad, but not that bad)

And the all time doozie:

"Surviving."

Surviving? Sounds like victim mode to me. "Oh woe is me. My life is terrible but I'm surviving."

Tony suggested a much more positive response, no matter how things actually are for you. He knew something back in 1990 that is a very important element of The Dirty Words way of being. We all know it's not good to have negative thoughts. We may have 50,000 thoughts (or more) per day and for many of us the majority are negative. That's not good. However, once we learn we have a "delete" button for brain programming, we realize that we can instantly let go of negative thoughts if we are aware of them. That's a great strategy.

The "Get To" Housekeeper

Since we're often not even aware of these negative thoughts, we need other strategies and tactics as well.

So, it's bad enough to have negative thoughts, especially if we are not aware of them. What's even worse is to birth a negative thought into our reality by actually speaking it. In doing so, we give it a boost of energy and literally bring it into being. It was just a negative thought. Once we speak it, it becomes a proclamation.

And what's worse than proclaiming a negative thought? It is proclaiming a negative thought about yourself. When we answer the question, "How are you?" with, "Not too bad," we are literally programming ourselves to be bad, just not too bad.

Tony's solution was to get into a habit of automatically answering with a positive response, no matter how things ACTUALLY are. So instead of "surviving" one could substitute the answer, "I'm great!"

In my case, I decided to take it up a notch by creating a standard answer that would certainly change my state, from wherever I was really at, to positive. I created a multi-word standard answer that would leave no doubt at all in anyone's mind (especially mine) that I truly was doing very well.

So, for years since, when I am asked, "How are you?" my response is often "Fantastic, incredible, if I felt any better, I would need to be restrained!" And every time I say that response, especially when I'm ACTUALLY feeling terrible, it immediately brings a smile to my face and literally changes my state.

And it usually changes the state of the person asking. Their response is often something like, "Wow, that's pretty good." And they'll often have a chuckle and say something like, "I wish I felt that good." Which of course opens up an opportunity for me to share with them that feeling good is a choice, and I just made the decision to feel great by responding with that answer.

I specifically remember one day in my office when I was a recording artist manager and I had just received some bad news about one of my artists being passed on by a major label. I was pretty disappointed because I had thought we were very close to doing a deal for a major recording contract that would literally change this artist's life.

The phone rang and the person on the other end dutifully asked, "How are you?" When I spewed out my usual response of, "Fantastic, incredible, if I felt any better, I would need to be restrained," I knew I was lying. The other person was taken aback and said, "Wow, what happened?"

So, instead of telling him about the bad thing that had happened, I had to quickly think of something good that was going on in my life. And when I did, I realized what a fantastic gift Tony Robbins had given me.

The "Get To" Housekeeper

Now, let's be clear. I don't use this standard answer in all situations. With close friends, or my spouse, or other family who really DO want to know how I am, people who I can share how I'm really feeling with, I will be honest and say how I'm really doing. Even with them though, if I want to share positive energy and perhaps help them feel good, I will revert to my standard response.

So, making a decision to become a "get to" person and eliminating each and every one of the "have to's" from your language will also literally change your state when you talk about cleaning the toilet, or anything else.

It all begs the question. Is the "get to" housekeeper's life a lot better because she chooses to use the phrase "get to?" Or does she use the phrase "get to" because she has such a good life? How is your life? Do you get to do most things, or do you have to do most things?

I'm guessing that you're using the words "have to" when you really mean "get to." It may be time for you to stop swearing!

CHAPTER 5

"SHOULDING" ALL OVER YOURSELF

Dirty Word #2 –
Should

Substitute Words –
Will
Am
Don't make the statement at all

BEST SUBSTITUTE –
Ask a question

How much success have you had using the word should? It's actually an awful, filthy word that can easily be eliminated from your vocabulary. Eliminating it can help you stop from making full statements or proclamations that don't serve you. It can especially help you stop shoulding all over the people around you and shoulding all over yourself as well.

"I should lose some weight."

"You should get your act together."

"I should really get on that project."

"You should stand up to your mother."

"I should start saving money."

"You should quit smoking."

"I should stop procrastinating."

"You should treat me with respect."

How have those kinds of proclamations been working for you?

Let's dissect each one and insert substitute words, change the statement into the form of a question, or just not say anything at all.

"I will lose some weight." "I am losing weight." Or, best yet, stop shoulding on yourself at all by just not talking about it. Just do it.

When you eliminate should from your vocabulary, you will automatically stop yourself from making such a damaging, demeaning statement such as "You should get your act together." It serves no purpose.

Most people, including those closest to you, will automatically reject your suggestion simply because you are using the word "should." No one likes to be told what they "should" do.

"I will get on that project." "I am getting right on that project."

If you really want to advise someone on the relationship with their mother, as dysfunctional as it may seem to you, the solution does not involve the word "should." Don't say anything, and if you feel compelled to, then use the question tactic to replace the word should. "Have you ever thought about standing up to your mother?" It's probably still not going to work, and at least there's a possibility.

"I will start saving money." "I am saving money."

"Have you thought about quitting smoking?" "How do you feel about being a smoker?" "Can I help you in any way to quit smoking?"

"I am no longer procrastinating." "I will stop procrastinating…when I get around to it." (That second version is thrown in for comic relief.)

"I am now asking you to treat me with respect."

You get the idea.

When we really take a close look at the word "should," it actually has no place, whatsoever, in our vocabulary. Can you catch yourself saying should? You will be amazed at how many times a day you use this word and how much of a positive impact eliminating this one simple word from your language can have on your life.

CHAPTER 6

I LOVE YOU BUT

Dirty Word #3 –
But

Substitute Words –
Only one substitute word that works in EVERY scenario:
And

If there is one word in the English language that is more pervasive that does more insidious damage than the word "but," I would challenge you to bring it forward. But is everywhere. And it is now time for you to "Get off your BUT" once and for all.

Imagine this marriage ceremony: It's a large wedding with 250 guests. The groom and his groomsmen are dressed impeccably, and the bride is simply stunning as she is escorted down the long aisle by her proud father as the organist plays "Here comes the Bride." It's a classic ceremony and the pastor gets to the vows.

"David, do you take Kristen to be your lawfully wedded wife, to have and to hold, in sickness and in health, as long as you both shall live?"

"I do, but …."

But????? But what? But, it's all subject to the terms of our prenuptial agreement? But, I reserve the right to change my mind if she gets too bitchy.

But, I just want to be clear that I'm not 100% sure.

Ridiculous certainly. And when we really start looking at how we use the word but, it is pretty crazy.

The fact is, that whatever we say in a sentence up to the point we say but, is 100% negated. Whomever we are talking to immediately dismisses anything said before "but" and in many cases doesn't even hear what is said before this filthy swear word.

"Son, I really love you, but, I'm really angry with you right now."

What does the boy hear? "Blah blah blah, I'm really angry with you right now."

"This has been a wonderful evening but, it's too bad it has to end."

What's wrong with, "Son, I really love you and I'm really angry with you right now"? "This has been a wonderful evening and it's too bad it has to end."

Of all the dirty words, this is by far the easiest to clean up. You can literally replace "but" with "and" in every conceivable situation. I challenge you to come up with a sentence using the word "but," where replacing it with "and" will not work. There is no such situation.

And is ALWAYS better than but. Try it. Oops…. That's our next dirty word.

CHAPTER 7

I'LL TRY TO BE THERE

Dirty Word #4 –
Try

Substitute Words –
Will
Won't
Will get back to you
Don't make the statement at all

BEST SUBSTITUTE –
Will or won't

Here's a tip: When you invite someone to an event and their response is, "I will try to be there" … THEY ARE NOT COMING. It's a lie. If they do actually show up, consider it a miracle.

Perhaps I'm exaggerating here AND (not but) for some reason, people will lie to your face about what they are going to or not going to do by simply using the word "try."

"I'll try." One of the most pervasive lies in our society.

This is the first of the dirty words so far that actually does have a legitimate use in language. As filthy as this word is in sentences described above, it is perfectly ok to use the word to encourage others, especially children, to make an effort to do something they are not sure they can do.

"Give it a try!" is a perfectly legitimate statement of encouragement. "You can do it. Just try." Even the response of someone making an earnest attempt, "I'm trying" is perfectly acceptable.

However, when we use the word "try" as a way of avoiding commitment, while acting like we are going to make an honest effort, when we know we have no intention to… that's foul language!

Especially when we make these lame proclamations about what we are going to do by using the word "try," we are completely disempowering ourselves. Don't ever use the word "try" when "will" or "won't" is the actual honest statement.

There's a wonderful demonstration of how awkward it is to "try" to do something instead of just doing it. Put a chair in the middle of a room. Ask your friend or loved one to sit in the chair. Then ask them to "try" to stand up. Take note of what happens.

The person will usually hesitate for a minute and then slowly start standing up. Stop them immediately and say, "No, don't stand up. TRY to stand up." Then watch as they sit back down and look very uncomfortable as they try to stand up without actually standing up. Trying to do something instead of actually doing it looks and IS very uncomfortable.

Can you imagine what a difference it would make at home, at work, throughout society if people stopped lying about what they are going to do or not do by using the word "try?"

Would Nike's long running and ultra successful marketing campaign have worked at all if it was, "Just try to do it?" I don't think so.

It's been said that there is no "try." If we decide to live a life of intention and honesty, there is no room for try. We simply do, or we don't. Both are acceptable.

Any good sales professional will tell you that getting a yes or a no is the objective. Obviously, a yes is best AND (not but) a no is so much better than a maybe. Top salespeople don't waste their time on time wasters. Sure, sometimes the maybe people who are "trying" to make a decision do eventually buy. In the meantime, a top salesperson will move on to other prospects and make several sales while an inexperienced sales person waits on the tire kickers.

Don't be a tire kicker. We only get one life to live. I'm not suggesting that you rush into important decisions without proper consideration and due diligence. I am suggesting that you be honest with your language and simply do or don't, instead of trying.

It's a form of procrastination. Don't let the "try" word divert you from making real proclamations that serve you. And don't bother "trying" to let friends down easy by telling them you are going to "try" to be there when you have no intention of coming.

And don't lie to yourself by saying that you are trying to lose weight, or quit smoking, or be a better person. Don't talk about what you are trying to do. Just do it and let your actions and results do the talking.

CHAPTER 8

I CAN'T

Dirty Word #5 –
I Can't

Substitute Words –
Will
Won't
Will get back to you
Don't make the statement at all

BEST SUBSTITUTE –
Will or won't

Interesting how the substitutes for Dirty Word #5 are exactly the same as Dirty Word #4.

There's a famous statement of philosophy that sums this up completely, "Whether you think you can or you think you can't, you are correct."

Can we possibly eliminate the word "can't" from our vocabulary? I think we can!

Some would say we "have to" (another dirty word) keep can't in our vocabulary because there are certainly many things we absolutely cannot do. Some things are simply "impossible."

That's interesting because I believe impossible is also a dirty word. I challenge you to consider that many, many aspects of our everyday life today were absolutely impossible 100 years ago, or 50 years ago, or 5 years ago. What we take for granted today as commonplace was not part of reality in the past.

"I can't possibly come visit you tomorrow as I live 3,000 miles away," would be a factual statement 100 years ago. Today when we say, "I can't come visit you tomorrow," it's actually a lie. We could come, if we decided to.

We say can't dozens of times each day when we really mean "won't."

"Oh, sorry I can't make it." Sometimes we follow that up with whatever lame excuse we decide to add on. My personal favorite is, "Oh, sorry I can't do that because my cat has a fur ball." How about, "My dog ate my homework?" "It's snowing out." "It's too sunny." "I'm too tired." "There's a full moon."

If you are not going to do whatever it is you are being asked, any excuse will work. Just don't lie and say you can't.

I know you don't want to hurt people's feelings by telling them the truth. So why not just lie and have them be disappointed later when the truth comes out?

Are you beginning to see how these dirty words screw up our lives?

We say we can't do this or that so many times each day we start to believe our own BS. And our kids are listening. And we also go so far as to tell other people what they can't do as well.

What if some of the great inventors, innovators, and leaders of history would have listened and paid heed to what they were told they can't do? What if they would have believed that certain things were indeed impossible?

Do you want to be a naysayer or a believer? Do you want to be a procrastinator or a doer? A large part of your answer to those questions involves paying attention to your language. Consider the opportunity that is presented before you, right here and now, to eliminate these dirty words from your vocabulary.

Or, maybe you simply can't.

CHAPTER 9

I HOPE IT WORKS OUT FOR YOU

Dirty Word #6 –
Hope

Substitute Words –
Believe it will
Pray

BEST SUBSTITUTE –
Trust

Hope as a dirty word??? Really?

"Hope" is probably the most fascinating dirty word. That's because when used correctly, it is one of the most beautiful and powerful words in our language. It is similar to the sacred words "God" or "Jesus." These are very beautiful and powerful words that when used "in vain" become sacrilegious and foul.

To have "hope" for all good outcomes for ourselves, our families, friends, circles of influence and all humanity is certainly appropriate, even laudable. Healthy hope, as we can refer to it here, includes a general intention for good. We all hope for peace on earth and goodwill toward all men. We encourage hope in our fellows and hold out hope for all that is outside our control or direct influence. We encourage our children to pursue their "hopes and dreams."

Where it gets a little dicey with the word hope is when we use it in scenarios that are NOT outside our control or influence.

"I hope things go well for you."

"I hope you get the help you need."

"I hope to be there."

"I hope you can get your act together."

"I hope we can work this out."

These are examples of hope being used as a deflection of responsibility, an unwillingness to be honest by not admitting our true intentions, and/or simply disempowering ourselves or others.

Let's examine a little closer and suggest substitute words:

"I hope things go well for you." Do we really just "hope" things are going to go well or is there something we can do to help? Instead of making this statement with an "unhealthy" hope in it, perhaps we want to make a

I HOPE It Works Out for You

commitment TO help. And if not, let's use more empowering replacement words such as "believe," "pray," (if appropriate for your or their faith) or best of all, in all situations, "trust."

"I trust things will go well for you." Isn't that just so much better than hoping?

"I hope you get the help you need." Again, how about deciding to offer specific help or asking if you can help? And if you are not prepared to make a commitment to help, then again "believing," "praying," or "TRUSTING" that the person will get the help they need are all better alternatives.

"I hope to be there." This is not healthy hoping. This is just like foul-mouthed "trying." How about, "I will be there." Or, equally honest and clear, "I won't be there." That can be followed by "I trust things will work out without me."

Are you getting the picture? Are you seeing how seemingly subtle changes and word substitutions can change how effective your communication is for sure, AND also can help you be more honest with yourself and others?

"I hope you get the help you need." Again, as we're about to spew out this garbage, perhaps we can re-evaluate and actually offer specific help. Or at least believe, pray, or trust instead of lamely hoping.

The Dirty Words

"I hope you can get your act together." This kind of statement is full of disempowerment just like "shoulding" all over those around us. "I believe you can get your act together." "I pray you can get your act together." "I trust you will get your act together." Three better choices that will actually instill confidence, not undermine.

"I hope we can work this out." Again, this is not healthy use of the word hope in situations where it is truly outside of our control. In this situation the appropriate statements are, "Let's work this out." "I believe we can work this out." "I pray we can work this out." "I trust we can work this out."

The dirty words issue is a little more complex than first meets the eye. Some words are just plain useless and suitable for elimination from our vocabulary. Others are ok in certain contexts. Don't hope to know the difference. Be careful, diligent, and intentional with your words. As your Mom always told you, "Watch your language!" Wise words indeed.

CHAPTER 10

I WISH I COULD HELP

Dirty Word #7 –
Wish

Substitute Words –
Believe it will
Pray

BEST SUBSTITUTE –
Trust

Wish is another tricky word that sounds perfectly fine until you really start to explore the issue of context. Very similar to hope, wish has its legitimate uses and can continue to be a part of your vocabulary if uttered carefully and appropriately.

Wishes are for wishing wells and wishing well. Wishing is not for use where we can take action, exercise influence, or make a difference. It is also not a substitute for honestly declining to take action or be there for someone.

The examples are similar to the hope scenarios:

"I'm wishing that things will go well for you."

"I'm wishing you get the help you need."

"I wish I could be there."

"I'm wishing and hoping you can get your act together."

"I wish we could work this out."

At first blush all these statements sound fine. And when we really think about it, the replacement words work much, much better.

"I believe that things will go well for you."

"I'm praying you get the help you need."

"I am going to be there." "I'm not going to be there." Either works!

"I'm praying and trusting you can get your act together."

"I trust we can work this out."

So, there's the initial list of 7 dirty words. These are the 7 words we suggest you don't say on television, or anywhere in any scenario. Feel free to consider other potential dirty words that may be candidates to eliminate from your vocabulary. Go to our web site or download our app to explore and discuss with others around the world.

CHAPTER 11

SPEAKING WITH INTENTION AND CLARITY

We're far enough along in the process now to start demonstrating to you how pervasive these words are in our language and provide some examples of how we string these dirty words together to completely disempower ourselves and others.

"Thanks for the invite. I will **try** to make it **but** I **have to** figure out my schedule. I **wish** I could commit but I **can't**. I **should** really be more organized with my schedule and I **hope** I can be."

Does that remind you of the construction worker dropping f-bombs seemingly every second or third word? It really is amazing how commonplace these dirty words have become.

Is this person really going to try to make it? Does she really have to figure out her schedule or is that her choice? She may indeed wish she could commit and that is something absolutely in her control, and certainly not impossible as the word "can't" suggests. Why make a statement about hoping she can become more organized and not just shut up and BE more organized?

These are the types of questions we can all ask ourselves when we notice ourselves using the dirty words.

How about this one from my own experience:

"Hey, thanks for the invite! I really **wish** I could be there **but** I **can't** because I **have to** take my son, Chris, to hockey."

Now here's what's really crazy about the above statement that spewed out of my cakehole when I got a cell phone call from a friend to join him for a beer with some friends at the local pub: It's all a lie, because I could join them if I wanted to and was choosing not to because I WANTED to take my son, Chris, to hockey.

And beyond crazy, here's what's really sad about this particular instance of poor choice of language: My son was listening to this from the back seat of the car with the phone on blue tooth speaker. How do you think he felt knowing that his Dad really "wished" he could be drinking with friends but "couldn't" because he "had to" take him to hockey? Which, of course, was not true at all!

Here's what I could have said if I was being honest AND extra careful NOT to use the dirty words:

Speaking with Intention and Clarity

"Hey, thanks for the invite. That would be really fun and I will take a rain check. I'm not going to be there because I GET TO take Chris to hockey!"

Wow, what a difference! That would put a smile on Chris's face and on my friend's as well. How insane is it that somehow in a lame attempt to let my friends down easy for turning down an invitation (which they were certainly not going to take personally anyway) I managed to lie to them and make my son feel bad simultaneously and for no good reason at all. And, I was completely unaware of what I had done!

Our lame choice of language can and does do REAL damage every single day. It's time for us all to make a firm decision to be very aware of the impact, positive and negative, of the words we choose and especially the proclamations that we make.

It's time to make a decision to begin communicating with intention and clarity.

Becoming aware of these and other words that don't serve us and starting to notice how we use them indiscriminately and without any consideration of their impact can be life altering. I've been conducting a workshop called "The Dirty Words" for over 20 years. Through these workshops, I've asked many hundreds of people from all walks of life to explore with me their list of "dirty words."

Through all those workshops, there have been other words suggested and debated about their qualification for

The Dirty Words

the "dirty words list." And there are indeed other words and certainly words in other languages that we all get to choose for ourselves, one way or the other, whether to continue to use them, eliminate them from our vocabulary, or adjust how we use them.

In every single workshop, these 7 words were unanimously upheld as dirty words. I encourage you to commit these words (have to, should, but, try, can't, hope, and wish) to memory and be very careful if and when you use them, or better still, eliminate them from your vocabulary.

One very important note: Do not start pointing out these words when others use them and correcting them, especially your spouse! Absolutely share this book and your new understanding of the dirty words and the power of the spoken word with your loved ones, friends, and associates.

Do not correct anyone on their use and/or misuse of these or any other words unless they come to understand what you've come to understand AND only if they ASK you to correct them. If they do decide to change their language, it can be fun for them to help you and you to help them by pointing it out when the words slip out.

CHAPTER 12

PROGRAMMING THE SUBCONSCIOUS MIND

Our ancestors used to believe the world was flat. Medical doctors used to smoke in their examination rooms and even endorse their favorite cigarette brand. Neuroscientists used to believe that brain damage was irreparable.

Today, we know that the brain is neuroplastic and we can literally re-wire our own brain through various forms of meditation and carefully crafted re-programming strategies and techniques being pioneered by renowned brain scientists like Dr. Joe Dispenza. Under scientifically monitored and carefully controlled conditions, thousands of people around the world are not only conquering life-long mental health challenges, such as chronic stress, anxiety, depression, and addiction through advanced forms of meditation, they are also healing their bodies as well as their minds.

Becoming aware of the potentially devastating effects of The Dirty Words in our day-to-day language can be just the first step on a very exciting journey of self-discovery and dramatic, life-altering change for the better. The concept of re-programing, literally, your brain and changing your life, and even your personality, has me very engaged and excited. I encourage you to apply what you are learning here about changing your language to change your life and then take further steps along a phenomenally exciting road of self-actualization.

Many thought leaders, not just today, going back decades and centuries, knew and know that only a small part of our life is lived on a conscious level. A very large percentage of our moment to moment existence is managed by our subconscious mind. Are you thinking about breathing right now? Are you consciously making sure your heart is beating? Are you aware of the complex digestion process that's taking place after every meal? Are you consciously generating the 50-70,000 thoughts that you have every day?

The answer to these questions is, of course not. There is so much going on at a subconscious level that in reality, we actually live our lives on a form of "autopilot." And research has proven that most of the programming or coding of our guidance system is put in place from age 0-7 and from then on, we buy into that programming and generally repeat the same patterns over and over and over again. And then we die.

The fantastic news is that just as you are able to learn consciously about The Dirty Words and make changes to your vocabulary, you can also learn to start reprograming your subconscious mind in the process. And what's really exciting is that the subconscious mind believes everything you tell it. When you use your imagination to focus on

Programming the Subconscious Mind

what you want, see the picture, and then tell yourself you have it now, your subconscious mind buys in. When you start to learn about how to more effectively re-program, re-wire, and tune up your brain, both on a conscious and subconscious level, all you've learned here about choosing your words very carefully will come in very, very handy!

Memorizing the seven dirtiest words (have to, should, but, try, can't, hope, and wish) and eliminating them from your vocabulary can be just the first step on an incredibly exciting path to a brand new, much happier, empowering, peaceful, and loving YOU! Use this book as a launching pad of exploration into the vast and plentiful world of self discovery and self improvement. The bookstores are overflowing, YouTube will serve you up video after video, and the search engines stand ready for all the key words you can type in.

When the student is ready, the teacher will appear. Decide, as you did by picking up this book, to be ready!

CHAPTER 13

A REAL-LIFE SUPERHERO

It does not matter what happens.

I have no idea if Christopher Reeve subscribed to that philosophy. He was an American born actor, film director, producer, screenwriter, author and equestrian. He achieved stardom for his acting achievements and is particularly well known for his motion picture portrayal of the DC comic book hero, *Superman*.

Reeve appeared in other critically acclaimed films such as *The Bostonians* (1984), *Street Smart* (1987), and *The Remains of the Day* (1993). He received a Screen Actors Guild Award and a Golden Globe Award nomination for his performance in the television remake of *Rear Window* (1998).

A striking physical presence, Christopher Reeve was a 6'4", athletic, handsome and successful actor with a beautiful wife and three children. He was living a dream life by most peoples' standards when on May 27th, 1995, his life suddenly changed forever.

Something happened.

He was enjoying one of his passions, horseback riding. He was originally allergic to horses after learning to ride in the 1985 film, *Anna Karenina*. He loved riding so much that he took antihistamines and his allergies soon disappeared.

Competing in an equestrian event ten years later in Culpeper, Virginia, he was suddenly thrown from his horse. He had fallen many times, as we all have in our lives, including many times off his horse while riding. This time was completely different.

The horse stopped suddenly and he was thrown forward and landed headfirst with his hands somehow tangled in the reigns. In an instant, his first and second vertebrae were shattered and he was instantly paralyzed from the neck down. He was unable to move and unable to breathe.

We've all experienced moments of terror. Usually those moments are just moments. Almost all of what we fear in life is not real. You may have heard the acronym for the word FEAR, False Evidence Appearing Real. Something happens and we are afraid, even gripped with fear, and within a moment, a minute or a few minutes, our fear subsides.

In this case, Christopher Reeve's fear did not subside. It quickly worsened from the gripping terror of flying off his horse with his hands entangled and unable to break his fall, to the sickening sound of his back breaking, to the shock of literally being unable to breathe.

A Real-Life Superhero

He could have died on the spot if paramedics had not arrived within three minutes to take immediate steps to clear his airway. He was taken first to the local hospital before being flown by helicopter to the University of Virginia Medical Center.

For the first few days after the accident, Reeve suffered from delirium, woke up sporadically and would mouth words to his wife Dana such as "get the gun" and "they're after us." After five days, he regained full consciousness and his doctor explained to him that he had destroyed his first and second vertebrae, which meant that his skull and spine were no longer connected. His lungs were filling with fluid and were suctioned by entry through his throat.

After considering his situation, believing that not only would he never walk again, but that he might never move a body part again, Reeve considered suicide. He mouthed to Dana, "Maybe we should let me go." She tearfully replied, "I am only going to say this once. I will support whatever you want to do because this is your life, and your decision. I want you to know that I'll be with you for the long haul, no matter what. You're still you. And I love you."

Note the lack of dirty words in Dana's proclamation to her husband.

Here was a man who seemingly "had it all." Suddenly, tragically most would say, his situation became so grave that he seriously considered suicide. Something had happened, and it seemed to matter A LOT.

The Dirty Words

It does not matter what happens.

It never matters what happens.

It only matters what you make it mean and how you choose to respond.

For Christopher Reeve, initially his interpretation of what happened and what he decided to make it mean was that perhaps it was not worth continuing to live. What had happened was so terrible, devastating, and terrifying that he considered the most drastic of responses: suicide.

And then something else happened. His wife chose to respond to the "tragedy" with an outpouring of unconditional love and renewed commitment to her marriage vows. She made a stunningly beautiful proclamation devoid of dirty words.

Reeve went through inner anguish in the ICU, particularly when he was alone during the long and agonizing nights. His approaching operation to reattach his skull to his spine (June 1995) "was frightening to contemplate.... I already knew that I had only a fifty-fifty chance of surviving the surgery," wrote Reeve.

Then, at an especially bleak moment, the door flew open and in hurried a squat fellow with a blue scrub hat and a yellow surgical gown and glasses, speaking with a Russian accent. The man announced that he was a proctologist and was going to perform a rectal exam.

A Real-Life Superhero

It was Robin Williams, reprising his character from the film *Nine Months*. Reeve wrote, "For the first time since the accident, I laughed. My old friend had helped me know that somehow I was going to be ok."

So, Christopher Reeve decided to choose a very different path from suicide.

He decided that, despite his dire diagnosis, he made the decision to fight for his own life and recovery. As a celebrity, he decided to dedicate his life to advocate for medical research in the field of spinal cord injury.

And, he made a powerful proclamation: "I will walk again."

I remember watching Christopher Reeve interviewed by Larry King on CNN. He was in a wheelchair, of course, and spoke in halting, partial sentences as he paused continuously allowing his ventilator to do its job.

It was an inspirational interview that brought tears to my eyes as he described how he had formed a foundation and was raising millions of dollars toward breakthrough research in the treatment of spinal cord injuries. He had travelled to Israel, a country that was then at the forefront of research in spinal cord injury, at the invitation of the Ministry of Foreign Affairs.

After meeting dozens of Israeli patients who had undergone ground-breaking recovery processes, Reeve was in awe and "almost overwhelmed." Israelis were very receptive to his visit, calling him an inspiration to all and urging him to never give up hope.

Because Reeve was constantly being covered by the media, he decided to use his name to put focus on spinal cord injuries. In 1996, he appeared at the Academy Awards to a long standing ovation and gave a speech about Hollywood's duty to make movies that face the world's most important issues head on.

He also hosted the Paralympics in Atlanta and spoke at the Democratic National Convention. He travelled across the country to make speeches, never needing a teleprompter or a script. For these efforts, he was placed on the cover of Time magazine on August 26, 1996.

Reeve was elected Chairman of the American Paralysis Association and Vice Chairman of the National Organization on Disability. He co-founded the Reeve-Irvine Research Center, which is now one of the leading spinal cord research centers in the world. He created the Christopher Reeve Foundation. The foundation, to date, has given more than $65 million for research and more than $8.5 million in quality-of-life grants.

I'll never forget watching television again a few years after I first saw Christopher Reeve on Larry King Live. Tears were again brought to my eyes as I watched in amazement as he stood partially erect and walked on a Locomotor Training treadmill that mimicked the movements of walking to help develop neural connections. This is a technology that has helped many people walk again by, in effect, re-teaching the spinal cord how to send signals to the legs to walk.

His proclamation had come true.

According to UC Irvine Medical Center, Christopher Reeve did more to promote research on spinal cord injury and other neurological disorders than any other person before or since.

The words we choose are very important. They often do reflect our reality. And when we use dirty words or are not careful with our choice of words, they can reflect quite the opposite. Even more importantly, our words, especially in the form of proclamations, can and do shape our reality.

Christopher Reeves and his wife Dana chose their words very carefully when they faced a life altering event. And in doing so, let's look at "what happened":

A man who pretended to be Superman in movies became a real-life superhero for people around the world. And not just average people like you and I, he became a real superhero for victims of spinal cord injury, and he was able to only because he was a victim himself.

Or was he? Perhaps victim is also a dirty word.

EPILOGUE

The Dirty Words as laid out in this book are intended as an opening to further self-discovery about how we impact on ourselves and others. Sometimes our impacts, positive and negative, empowering and destructive, loving and hateful, are obvious. Mostly, and sadly, they are not. We don't pay enough attention to our choice of words and often our thoughts and words are recklessly flowing from subconscious programming that we are simply oblivious to.

So, completing this book creates an opening for you. As the official companion book of The Questions Experience, I invite you to explore further, and possibly go much deeper along your own personal path of self discovery. I invite you to answer The Questions, eight compelling queries that came to me in the form of what I believe is a divine intervention at a time in my life when my faith was very much in question. The Questions were written by hand in less than five minutes with very little conscious thought on my part. Since that day, over 20 years ago, I've been using The Questions in both personal and business coaching sessions, as well as in experiential workshops for individuals, corporate team building, non-profit organizations and even in an evangelical church setting.

The Questions have had a strikingly positive, often transformational impact on ALL of the more than 1,000 people so far, at the time of this writing, who have taken the time to answer them. My personal engagement with them in simply coaching people about their answers both in one-on-one and workshop settings has been 100% successful in at a minimum delivering an awakening or epiphany for every single person I've worked with. In the vast majority of cases, individual and workshop participants report a "major breakthrough" in the process of answering further questions about their answers to The Questions.

The Questions Experience is now a movement with certified coaches, speakers, trainers, pastors and other spiritual leaders being trained as Questions Experience Practitioners so that more and more people around the world can "find their own answers" through these beautiful questions.

I invite you to answer The Questions, and make sure you don't use any "Dirty Words." Just answering them alone, without any further coaching or group work, will benefit you. If you are courageous enough to go deeper and allow others to challenge you on your answers, I promise you an experience that will inspire you. It's no accident that you decided to read this book.

To learn more about The Questions Experience, including how to have The Questions sent to you, have a one-hour coaching session around your answers, attend a Questions Experience workshop in your area, bring The Questions Experience to your workplace, volunteer organization, or place of worship, or to find out how to apply to become a Certified Questions Experience Practitioner, please visit https://thequestionsexperience.com

ACKNOWLEDGEMENTS

My e-mail signature says, "In Gratitude" and that is how I live. I am grateful to be here on this planet living this amazing roller coaster life!

So, to say I am grateful to be blessed with the opportunity to write and publish this book is an understatement. And, I am grateful to have the opportunity to document just a few of the wonderful people in my life who've helped make it happen.

Thank you to my publishing team at Hyperspace Internet Technologies, Inc. The team coordinator, Robbi Gunter challenged me to finish what I started by actually publishing the book and is playing a wonderful roll in spreading The *Dirty Words* and *The Questions Experience* around the world.

Thank you to my family, starting with my deceased Mom and Dad, Edith and Joe Lennon, my siblings Loreen Lennon, Rob Lennon, and Leeann Lennon and their families. Thank you to my deceased Uncle Ned Stephans, Auntie Shirley and Uncle John Millenchuk, Myrna McCowan, my wife Dee Lennon, and my wonderful boys David Lennon, Michael Lennon, and Christopher Lennon.

Thank you to Ray Lautt and all my school teachers and to my mentors Terry Willox, The Honorable Preston Manning, the late Terry Clements, the late Staff Sergeant Ron Steele, the late Ken King, and my hero and surrogate Dad, John Elson.

Thank you to my buddies over the years Barry Knobel, Ben Jonsson, Brian Mumby, John Berry, Garet Bonn, Gary Hubka (Tokyo Rose), Les Dombroski, Ritch Winter, Doug Main, Chris Pelonis, Bob Baker, Ken Cline, the late Derrick Boyd, Keith Turner, Chester Aldridge, Sidney Schultz, Adrian Bohach, Alex Miller, Brian Taylor, David Meunier, Mark Powell, Vic Lebouthillier, and Darrell Greenman.

Thank you to these special people who have encouraged and supported me particularly around The Dirty Words and The Questions Experience: Ron Evans, Dr. Geoff Tunnicliffe, Karren Gauvin, Marina Geronazzo, Samantha Milligan, Kirei Yasunori and Cristi McMurdie.

Thank you to my inspirational guides Tony Robbins, the late Dr. Wayne Dyer, Esther Hicks, and Dr. Joe Dispenza. Special thanks to my sister in Christ, Carmen Millar.

And, all glory to Jesus Christ, our Holy Savior.

ABOUT THE AUTHOR

Randy Lennon is an entrepreneur with decades of experience, having founded and built successful enterprises in the fields of newspaper publishing, television and radio, recording artist management, retail, advertising and marketing, and the Internet. Randy has also worked as a police officer, as a regional and national television and radio talk show host, as an actor in a situation comedy pilot co-starring with the late Fred Willard, and a special advisor to the leader of a major national political party in Ottawa. His recording artists have won US Gold and Platinum albums as well as the Juno Award in Canada.

Founder of the Spruce Grove Examiner newspaper at age 19, Randy built and grew the company to a chain of four weekly newspapers. Over 40 years later, The Examiner continues to serve the Edmonton, Canada community as a trusted newspaper brand. As Chairman of the Privatization Committee of the board of directors of Access Television Network, Randy oversaw the first successful privatization of a public television broadcaster in North America.

As a television and radio personality, speaker and trainer in areas of personal growth and self development, and as a business mentor and angel investor, Randy has a passion for empowering others. As the founder of The

Questions Experience, he has helped more than 1,000 people, through one-on-one coaching and workshops, determine what stops them, and how to shift toward pursuing their true calling in life. The Dirty Words training is part of The Questions Experience workshop.

NOTES

NOTES

NOTES

NOTES

NOTES

NOTES

NOTES

NOTES

CPSIA information can be obtained
at www.ICGtesting.com
Printed in the USA
LVHW051921230920
666903LV00005B/1180

9 780578 718897